CONTENTS

PETS

REPTILES

HORSES AND PONIES

CONTENTS

INTRODUCTION

Are you ready to learn how to draw some of the coolest creatures on the planet? From a cute, fluffy rabbit to a deadly crocodile, this book will teach you all the techniques you need to create lifelike drawings that leap off the page!

Soon, you will be able to use these methods to draw any creature you like – and create an amazing habitat for them. Sharpen your pencil and let's get started!

THE BASICS

DRAWING

Start your drawings with simple guidelines, before fleshing them out with detail.

Guidelines

Build up the general shape of your subject with guidelines. I have drawn the guidelines quite heavily to make them easy to follow, but you should work faintly with a hard pencil.

Detail

Use a softer pencil to develop the character and details. You may find that you do not follow the guidelines exactly in places. That's fine – they are only a rough guide.

Shading and texture

Carefully erase the guidelines and mistakes. Then add shading and texture with a soft pencil.

INKING

For a bold look, go over the outlines with ink. Wait for the ink to dry thoroughly, then erase all the pencil marks.

Felt-tip pen outlines

The easiest inking method is to use a felt-tip pen. If you plan to add paint later on, make sure your pen is waterproof.

Brush outlines

For a more graceful effect, use a fine-tipped watercolour brush dipped in ink.

COLOURING

Although I use watercolours in this book, the main principles are the same for any materials – start with the shading, then add in markings and textures, and finally work your main colours over the top.

Felt-tip colouring

Felt-tip pens produce bright, vibrant colours. Work quickly to avoid the pen strokes remaining visible.

Coloured pencils

Coloured pencils are the easiest colouring tools to use, but you have to take great care to blend the colours to achieve a good finish.

Watercolours

The subtlest effects can be achieved with watercolour paints. It is best to buy watercolour paints as a set of solid blocks that you wet with a brush. Mix the colours in a palette, or on an old white plate.

PETS

DRAWING FUR

Whether you are drawing a long- or short-haired animal, you can never show every hair – instead you need to simplify and suggest the texture of the fur. Generally, the more marks you use, the scruffier the animal will look.

Short fur detail

Long fur detail

Once the basic outline is right you can start to add details for the fur. The fur over the top of the head is usually shorter than that under the chin, and the fluffiest hairs are often found in the ears. Indicate the direction in which the fur flows over the body with simple marks.

Short fur

Long fur

The important thing to start with is to make the animal convincing before going into any detail. Where fur is very long, it can be sketched in as a broad shape.

Short fur inking

Long fur inking

To ink in the marks, use long, swift flowing strokes of the brush or pen and work around the whole drawing quickly. Don't feel that you need to ink every mark or outline – if the fur is very fine or pale, it will need no more than a few wispy strokes.

GOLDEN RETRIEVER

Golden retriever dogs are well-loved pets in many homes. They are gentle, loyal and very intelligent. They also love playing in water! Their thick golden coat has two different types of fur – a soft underneath layer that helps to keep the dog warm, and a shaggier outer layer that is water-resistant to keep the dog dry.

1 Dogs come in all shapes and sizes, but the first steps for drawing them are quite similar – it's just the proportions that change. The golden retriever has quite a large, long body with a relatively small head. Draw the body and head as simple shapes, an oval and a circle, with a space in between.

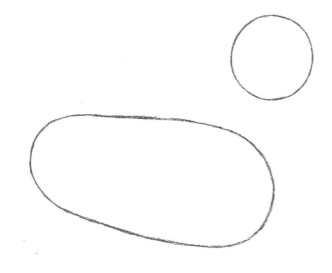

2 Now join the head to the body with curving lines that show the neck leaning forwards. Draw the upper part of the rear leg as a broad shape that also forms the dog's rump. Then mark the front edges of the legs, taking care to make them the right length.

3 Finish the leg guidelines and add paw shapes. The tail is broad, curving to a point. Draw a roughly triangular muzzle and mark a centre line that curves over the top of the head. This will help you to position the eyes on either side of the line, and the ears on the sides of the head.

4 Add more detail to the face and draw some individual toes on each paw. Now start work on the coat. Show the shagginess of the coat with simple outlines and curving marks around the neck to suggest the direction of growth.

5 With all the guidelines in place you can now refine the drawing with a sharp pencil. Work on the face, aiming for a friendly expression. Add some more detail to the coat, mainly on the underside of the animal, behind the legs and around the neck and chest.

6 To bring out the golden retriever's colouring, I used a pale yellow-brown ink for most of the outlining. I used black for the dark eyes, nose and mouth. Then I watered down some black ink to add detail to the paws and shadow areas.

7 For the shading I mixed some purple with dark yellow paint. I shaded the parts of the dog that would be in shadow with the light coming from the upper left. I also used this paint for some deep shadows in the coat, making sure my brush strokes followed the growth of the fur.

CLEVER DOGS

Golden retrievers are too friendly to be good guard dogs! But their intelligence means they can be trained to do many useful jobs for humans. These include working as guide dogs for blind people, or sniffing out people trapped after natural disasters such as earthquakes. Because they are such good swimmers, golden retrievers are also used for water rescues and life-saving!

ANIMAL FACTS

8 The colouring of most animals is not the same all over, and the golden retriever is no exception. Its colouring is richer along the back, the legs and parts of the head – generally where the coat is least fluffy. I painted these parts first with orange mixed into dark yellow, then softened the edges with a dampened tissue before the paint dried.

9 To tie all the colours together I used a watery yellow-brown mix to wash over the entire dog.

10 For the finishing touches I added a few more spots of purple shade under the neck, inside the legs and on the paws. Then I used diluted white ink to paint on some highlights to make the fur shiny, and to bring out the features of the face and paws.

CAT

Cats have strong, flexible bodies. They walk lightly on their toes, and they are very agile and quick-footed. Like wild cats such as lions and tigers, many pet cats are hunters. They often catch their prey after dark, helped by their excellent night vision.

1 The view I have chosen shows the cat looking over its shoulder, so the circle that forms the head is placed almost centrally above the larger oval shape of the body. Make sure you leave a gap between the two shapes.

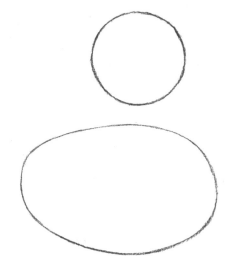

2 Join the two shapes with a long, arching neck line on the outer edge. For the front leg, continue the neck line down, curving inwards. At the rear end, form the shape of the upper leg and rump, then draw the leg shapes in between. The front legs should be wider than the rear.

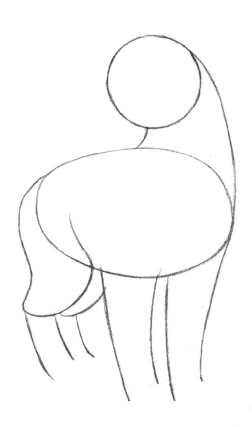

CAT TONGUES

Pet cats spend many hours each day grooming –
licking their coats to keep them clean. Their
tongues are rather like mini-hairbrushes!
The surface of the tongue is covered with
tiny, backwards-facing spines, which clean
and untangle the fur as the cat licks.

ANIMAL FACTS

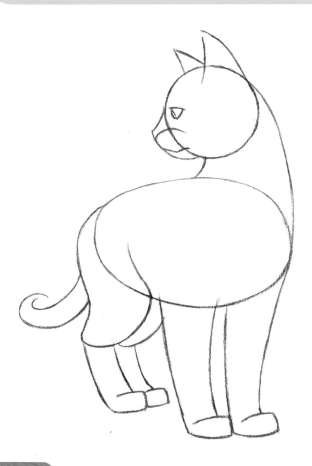

3 Add the ears and the basic lines of the face and suddenly your drawing looks like a cat. Some feet shapes and a low-slung tail complete the basic outline.

4 Now put in some shaping and markings to the head and toes on the paws. Draw lines around the cat's body to guide you for the fur markings.

5 As you add detail to the drawing, pay attention to the shapes of the shoulders and hips. Make the outlines furry as you go. Draw character into the face and head, and put some striped markings across the body.

6 For the inking stage, I used a fine brush and black ink to create a furry texture with many fine strokes. I did not erase the pencil drawing because I wanted to follow the guidelines for the stripes at the next (painting) stage.

7 After painting the stripes in dark brown, I erased the pencil work. Then I added some orangey colour to the legs and feet. Once dry, I painted on some shadow in purpley-grey, then I washed blue-grey over the whole body. I used the same blue-grey to paint textural marks to give a rough, shaggy look. Then with watered-down white ink I brought out more of the shaggy texture as well as the highlights in the eyes, ear hairs and whiskers.

RABBIT

The rabbit's most noticeable features are its long ears. It also has large, powerful back legs which it uses to hop – and to run very fast when necessary. Pet rabbits are often kept in hutches, but some are trained to live freely in people's homes as 'house rabbits'.

1 Start with two overlapping shapes, a circle and a large oval, for the rabbit's distinctive body shape. Add a smaller circle sitting on top of the first one for the head.

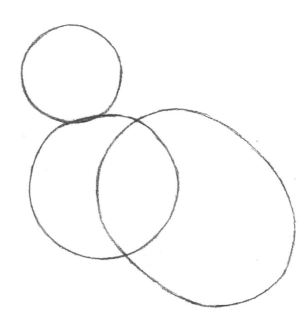

2 Draw two large teardrop shapes for the ears. Then add the legs as simple shapes, the front legs sitting underneath the body's circle and the hind legs a long way back under the oval.

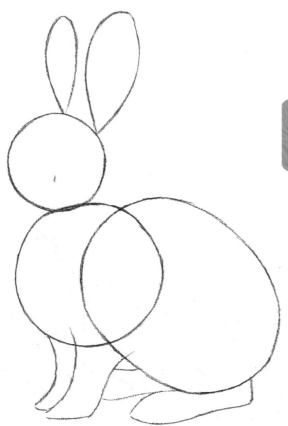

3 Draw two oval shapes in front of the head for the muzzle, with a nose in between. Join the ears to the head and mark in the eye. Shape the back end, adding a little tail.

4 Work on the outline details around the head and eye. Draw some individual toes on the feet.

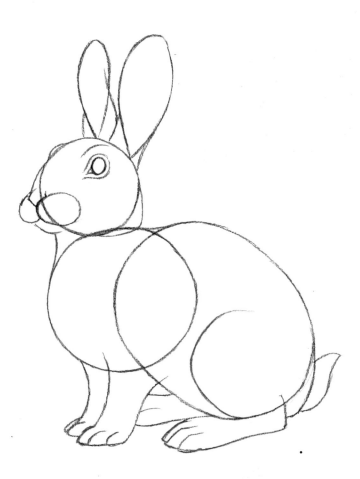

THUMPING AND HOPPING

In the wild, rabbits are food for animals such as foxes and birds of prey. They warn other rabbits of danger by thumping their powerful hind legs on the ground. If necessary, they hop away in zig-zags to try to confuse and outwit their attacker.

ANIMAL FACTS

5 Now work over the whole drawing to make the rabbit look as soft and friendly as you can. I chose to give mine bold black and white markings, so I drew the outlines of the black patches to guide me at the inking stage.

6 Although this rabbit has patches of solid black, I did not want to use ink for all of these areas because this would make for a flat and lifeless picture. I reserved the black ink for the very darkest parts, and for some delicate outlines around the rest of the animal.

7 For the delicate shading I used a brown-blue mix, which is less dull than plain grey. I built up the shade in two or three layers, using light marks. For the black, I used a mix of very dark blue and dark red. I built up the black with several layers, blending it into the black ink patches. Some spots of pink and yellow-brown added detail to the feet, ears and nose. For a few highlights on the fur, I used diluted white ink.

GARDEN SCENE

You can build on the skills you have learned in this chapter by putting your favourite pets into a scene. Here I have chosen the cat and the dog.

1 After playing around with various ideas on scrap paper, I settled on this composition. I decided to stand the cat on a raised surface, and to make the animals appear to be looking at each other. I reworked it, still at a small scale. Doing rough versions like this can save a lot of time later.

2 I decided that my pencil rough looked a little unbalanced, so I added a rail on the left-hand side of the picture. Then I roughly applied shade and colour with watercolours. I restricted my palette to greens and yellowy browns, with some touches of blue here and there.

3 Once I was happy with the colouring, I went on to develop the light and shade. Then I used black and white ink to strengthen the outlines and highlights. In this small rough I have established the main areas of light and shade which will help with the larger-scale artwork.

4 On a large sheet of good paper, sketch in the guidelines for the final artwork. The aim here is to establish a loose framework for all the different parts of the picture – the lines of the decking and fencing, and the rough shapes of the animals.

5 With the framework and positions established, you can now develop the shapes, avoiding too much detail until all the necessary guidelines are in place.

6 With a fine pencil and eraser, work over all the important details, erasing any confusing guidelines as you go. I left the fine detail that I would need for the next (inking) stage.

7 I used dark brown ink to avoid the outlines being too harsh. I watered it down to outline distant and less important features. For the dog, I used a golden brown ink. Once the ink was dry, I erased all the pencil work.

8 Using my colour rough as a guide, I painted in the shadows and shading using purple-brown and blue-green. Then I added in the colours, leaving no white paper showing. I strengthened some of the colours as necessary, before adding highlights. I also mixed white with different greens to add texture to some of the plants.

REPTILES

TIPS AND TRICKS

DRAWING FEET

IGUANA FEET

The feet of the iguana are quite complicated, with fingers of different lengths.
Draw a palm shape, then mark the rough positions and lengths of the fingers.

Mark the joints as circles along the length of the finger lines.

Flesh out the fingers and draw the claws on the ends.

CROCODILE FEET

A crocodile's feet are rather like human hands.
Draw the shape of the palm and then a curve that marks the length of the fingers.

Add pointed shapes spreading outwards for the fingers.

Flesh out the fingers, add webbing in between and draw the short claws at the tips.

ADDING SCALES

When you draw a whole creature, don't try to fill in every scale.

These examples are not finely detailed, but still capture the effect of the different scales.

Tortoise

Crocodile

Snake

CROCODILE

The biggest and heaviest of all living reptiles, the crocodile is a fearsome hunter. It has powerful jaws and sharp teeth for grabbing prey. The scales on the underside of the crocodile are small and smooth. On its back, it has large, ridged scales that act as protective armour.

1 Start with a long, smooth curve that runs right around the crocodile's powerful tail and body. Then add a neat circle in front as a guide for the crocodile's unusual neck shape.

2 Add the jaws and the beginnings of the legs. Now the crocodile starts to take shape.

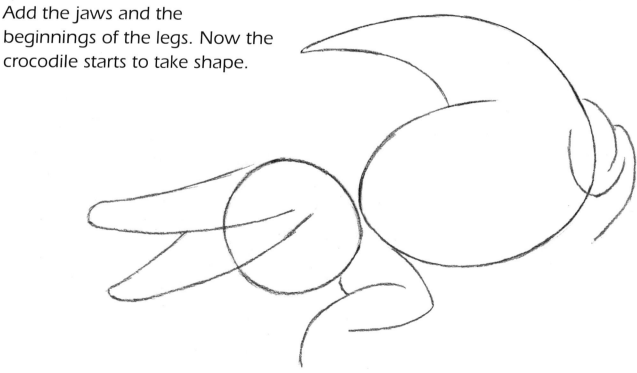

3 Join up the head, neck and body with a few lines and add eyebrow ridges. Then sketch in the feet – five toes on the front feet, four on the back. Start to map out the ridges on the back, drawing the outer edges and the centre line.

4 Now flesh out the details – the lines of the mouth and teeth, the claws and webbed toes. Fill in the guidelines for the back ridges. They should be evenly spaced on the body, but they should get smaller along the tail.

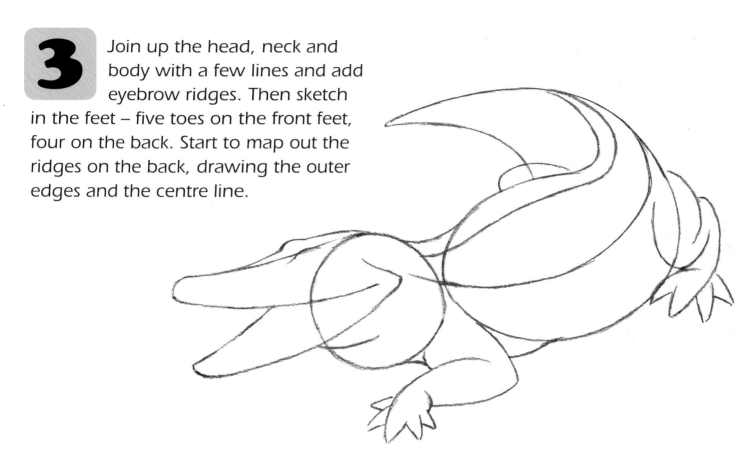

5 This is where the fun starts! Now that the guidelines are all in place you can work up the details with your pencil, refining and reshaping the drawing wherever necessary. You can erase the guidelines as you go.

6 For this example, I did most of the inking with a brush. I also used a fine felt-tip pen for the delicate details of the teeth. For the shadow and texture of the crocodile's underside, I used criss-cross shading to follow the curve of the rounded body.

7 The first stage of painting is the shading. Decide on a direction for the light to come from – here it is upper right. Mix up a neutral grey colour. Try to avoid using black paint – it's much better to mix up a grey from other colours, for example, purple with a bit of brown and blue.

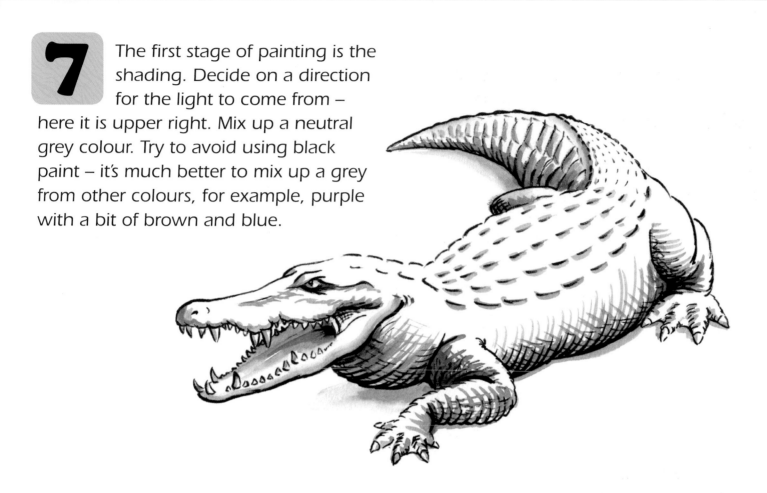

STEALTH CROC

A swimming crocodile can be hard to spot in rivers and lakes. The only parts that remain visible above the surface of the water are the crocodile's nostrils, eyes and ears, which are on the highest part of its head. The rest of the crocodile's massive body is hidden beneath the surface.

ANIMAL FACTS

8 For the crocodile's markings I mixed up a dark grey-green (again using no black paint) and painted broad, rough stripes down the back. I used the tip of the brush for more delicate dabs and spots.

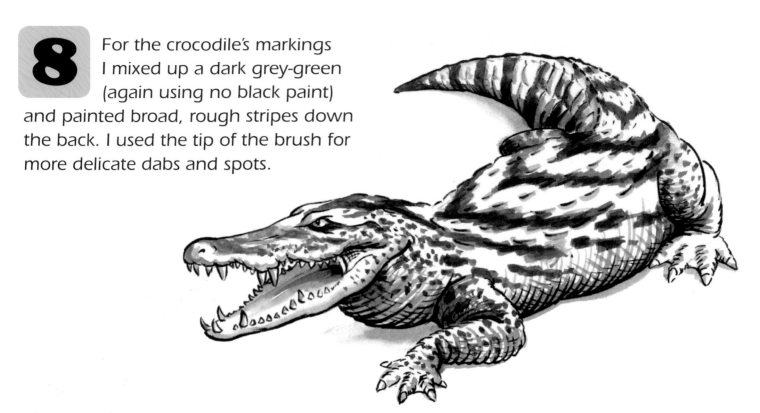

9 Paint flat colours over the top of the shading and markings. This will blend all the paintwork together, softening the edges. I used two colours, mid-green for the back and yellow-brown for the undersides. Make sure the paint is not too thick or dark, or the layers underneath will not show through.

10 Now it's time to add tiny spots of colour for highlights, on the eyes and claws, for example. Look hard at your picture to see if any areas need brightening. For highlights, you will need some white paint or ink, or you could use a sharpened piece of chalk. The highlights bring out the shine on a subject and show up its texture.

IGUANA

The iguana is a large lizard that lives in Central America and the Caribbean. Male iguanas can grow to up to two metres (six feet) in length. The iguana uses its sharp eyes to look for food. If attacked, it lashes out with its long, whip-like tail.

1 Draw a long egg shape for the iguana's body, then the outer edge of the tail flowing smoothly on from its back. The head should be drawn separately and is roughly triangular in form.

2 Now join the head and body with curving lines to make the iguana's shape. The tail should get narrower towards the tip. Start to work on the legs by carefully marking the outer edges.

3 Iguanas have strange feet, so spend some time getting them right. For now the toes can be simple lines. You can also draw a branch for the iguana to sit on.

4 A line down the back will be your guide for the iguana's spikes. Add more detail to the head. To help with the complicated knuckles in the feet, draw small circles on each of the joints.

5 Now you can add the finishing touches to your pencils. Follow the guidelines drawn in stage 4 as you add detail to the feet.

6 Use a thin brush or a fine pen for the delicate lines of the spikes, claws and fingers. You can ink more heavily in some of the shadow areas and add texture to the branch.

TAIL TRICKS

If an attacker grabs hold of an iguana's tail, the iguana has a cunning trick. It allows its tail to drop off and then runs away! In time, a perfect new tail will grow in its place.

ANIMAL FACTS

7 For creatures of more than one colour, try to blend the colours into each other. This effect is tricky with felt-tips, but quite easy with coloured pencils. If you are using paint, you should work the two colours together while wet.

RIVER SCENE

Now you have mastered drawing individual reptiles, it's time to experiment with putting them into a natural scene.

1 The first stage of developing a scene is a rough pencil drawing on scrap paper. This is to work out the sizes and positions of all the elements in the scene. Don't worry if you make lots of changes and do lots of erasing before you are happy with the result.

2 Before moving on to a more detailed artwork on good paper, you can plan your colours and shading by quickly colouring in your rough drawing. The idea of a colour rough is to find out what does and doesn't work, before you start on the final artwork.

3 To complete the colour rough, I have used a black felt-tip to define the outlines and deep shadows, as well as some white ink for highlights. I also decided to add some more foliage in the foreground and to darken some of the shading in the background and river.

4 On a fresh sheet of good paper, draw guidelines for the main shapes that make up the picture. Work across the whole surface without getting into details. Think of the plants as broad shapes.

5 Gradually build up the detail. Use the skills you have learned in this chapter to develop the animals, then work on the surrounding elements. Draw in the details of the foreground plants, but make those in the background more sketchy. You can still make changes – I decided to alter the plants in the foreground from those in my colour rough.

6 Use a sharp pencil to refine the whole drawing. Pay attention to the characters of the animals. Try to keep the individual shapes of the plants clearly defined. Erase any confusing marks and guidelines.

7 It is a good idea to start inking in the elements that are closest to the front of the picture, then work backwards. Use strong, confident strokes to make the plants and leaves graceful. Marks in the background should be finer and less distinct.

8 Start with the shading in a neutral colour, as you did with the crocodile on page 35. Vary the colours of green for the different plant types. I have used brighter colours around the iguana and duller colours near the crocodile.

HORSES
and Ponies

BODY SHAPE

Here we look at the horse's body structure in three different ways.

This diagram shows the way that a horse's body can be measured in head lengths. An average horse is about three head lengths tall at the shoulder. Its torso (main body) is also three head lengths long. However, these proportions can be different for horses of different breeds and ages.

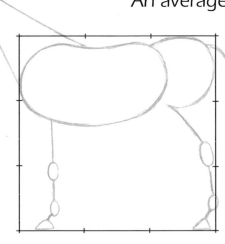

Proportions

This skeleton view of a horse should help you to make sense of the joints. The shoulderbones push forwards from the chest and the hips angle backwards. Notice where the joints are found in the legs.

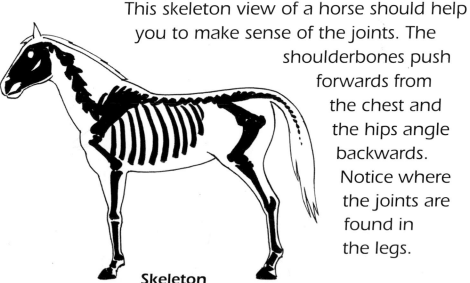

Skeleton

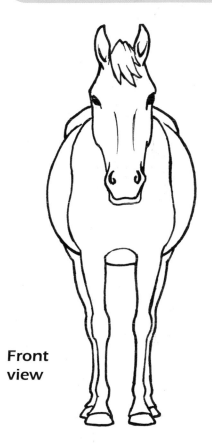

Front view

Viewed from the front, you can see that the shoulders are narrow, the hips wider and the belly rounded and broad. Note how close together the legs are on the ground.

THOROUGHBRED

A thoroughbred is a breed of horse used for racing, jumping and other equestrian sports. Thoroughbreds are usually agile, quick and lively.

1 Begin by drawing a large oval with a flat top. This is the main part of the horse's chest and belly. Add a small circle for the head, and a long curve off the animal's rear end for its rump. Leave enough space on the paper for the legs and tail.

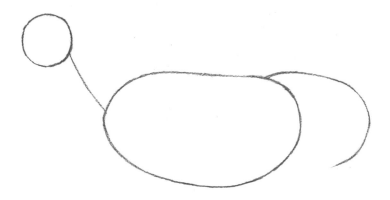

2 Draw the cone shape of the muzzle and then add a line for the back of the neck, arching over the head. Sketch in the long, thin curves of the legs, which become narrower towards the feet.

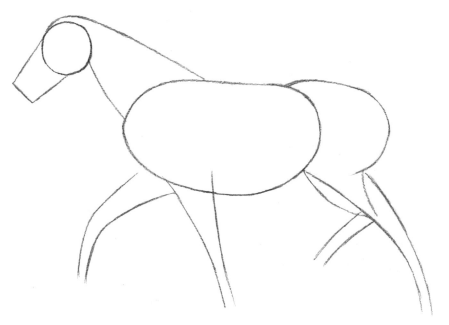

3 Horses' legs have visible joints, which look quite knobbly. It's a good idea to draw fairly large ovals on the legs for each joint, taking care to place them correctly. Sketch out the mane and tail as simple shapes without texture or detail.

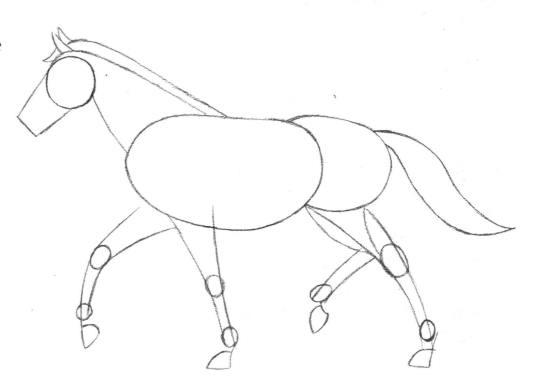

4 Now that the guidelines are finished, you can start on the details. Draw the main features of the face and the shape of the headcollar. Work on the upper legs. Note the bulky shoulder area at the front of the chest above the leading (front) leg.

5 Work on the detail using a sharp pencil and an eraser. Make the body curves smooth and graceful, and pay attention to the muscles and joints of the legs. Work on the head and headcollar and add some flowing texture to the mane and tail.

6 Once you are happy with your outlines, it's time to ink them in. Use fine, confident strokes. Move the paper around on your desk to allow your arm to work freely. When the ink is dry, all the pencil work can be erased to leave a clean outline.

7 You can break the colouring process down into stages. For this horse, I decided to start with the dark markings. I mixed dark brown and blue to make black. Where the markings blend into the upper leg, I used a dampened brush to soften the hard edge of the paint marks. I also added some shading to the ankles and hooves.

FAMOUS HORSES

Thoroughbreds are ridden by people in a wide range of sporting events. Many are trained to be racers – either on flat courses with no jumps, or in races with fences and ditches. The most successful of these horses have become racing legends, with names such as Seabiscuit, Red Rum and Desert Orchid.

ANIMAL FACTS

8 To add shading to the body, I mixed up a warm dark brown colour. I used this colour for the darkest areas, under the belly and inside the legs. Where the shading was less dark, I watered down the paint. Then I softened the edges of the painted areas with a wet brush and clean tissue paper.

9 Once the shading is complete, wash the main colour on in broad strokes. Keep the paint flowing and do not allow any hard edges to become dry as you work. When the area is covered, allow it to dry completely.

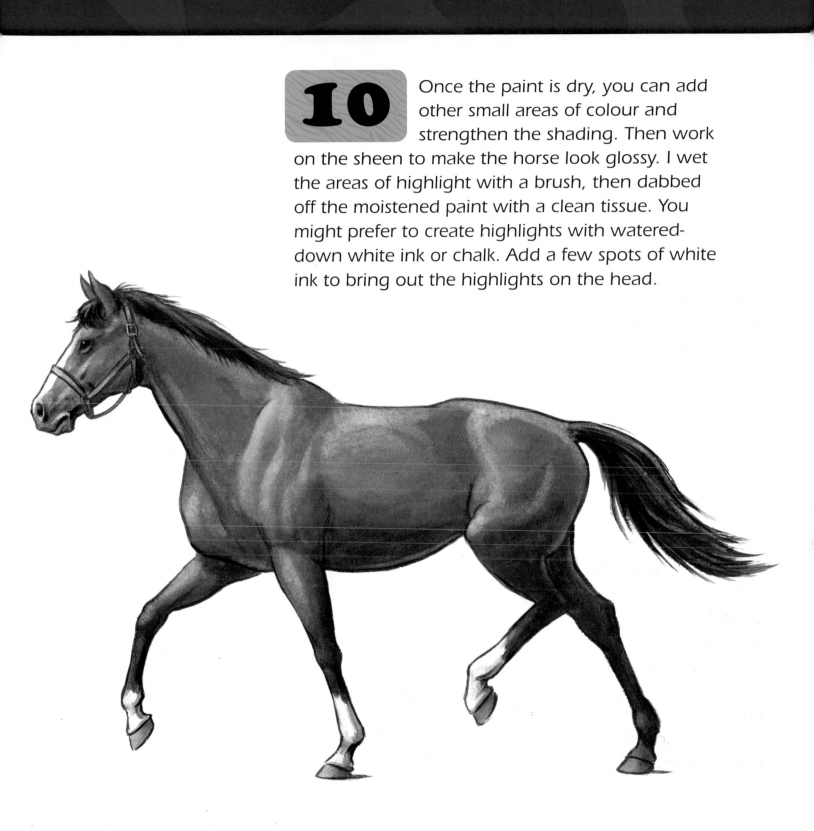

10 Once the paint is dry, you can add other small areas of colour and strengthen the shading. Then work on the sheen to make the horse look glossy. I wet the areas of highlight with a brush, then dabbed off the moistened paint with a clean tissue. You might prefer to create highlights with watered-down white ink or chalk. Add a few spots of white ink to bring out the highlights on the head.

FOAL

A foal is a baby horse, up to one year old. Foals have very long legs and small, slim bodies. Their manes and tails are short. After its first birthday, a foal is known as a yearling.

1 Although a foal is much leaner than a fully-grown horse, you start with a similar oval for the chest and belly. Add a circle for the head and a long curve off the animal's rear end for its rump.

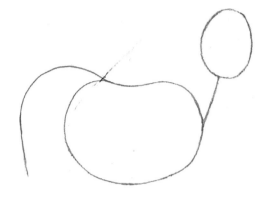

2 Draw in the muzzle and the neck, arching over the head. Sketch in the legs, which are very long and thin on a foal.

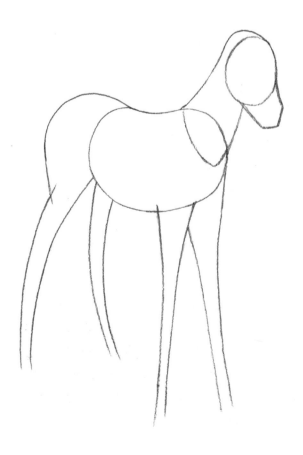

LONG LEGS

When a foal is born, its legs are almost as long as they will be when it has grown into an adult horse. Unlike human babies, foals use their legs almost straight away. A foal will be standing within an hour of birth, and by one day old it will be trotting and galloping next to its mother.

ANIMAL FACTS

3 Draw the head as a roughly rectangular box at this stage. The knees are very knobbly and the tail and mane are short. To place the legs firmly on the ground, draw a neat shape on the floor to guide you.

4 Now draw in the main features of the face and the ears. Work on the upper legs, bringing out the curves of the foal's muscles. Add some detail to the hooves.

5 Continue working on the detail of the head, mane and short tail. Make the body curves smooth and pay attention to the joints on the foal's long legs.

6 To give a softer feel for this young animal, I decided on coloured ink for part of the outline. I used a yellow-brown colour for the body and upper legs, and black ink for the darker parts.

7 Although the nose is as dark as the legs and tail, it is more grey in colour. A young horse is not as sleek and shiny as an adult. To give a sense of the fluffier coat, I painted some short, soft strokes on the foal's body.

WILD PONY

Wild ponies are usually quite broad and sturdy animals, with short legs. Their coats are fairly coarse and thick to keep them warm in winter, and they have long manes and tails. These hardy little ponies have to be able to survive all weathers.

1 This wild pony is a much sturdier creature than the others in this chapter, so make the oval of the body extra deep and rounded. Add a circle for the head.

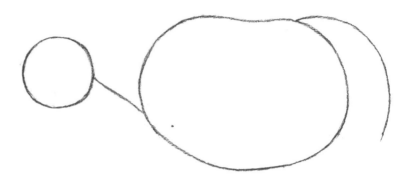

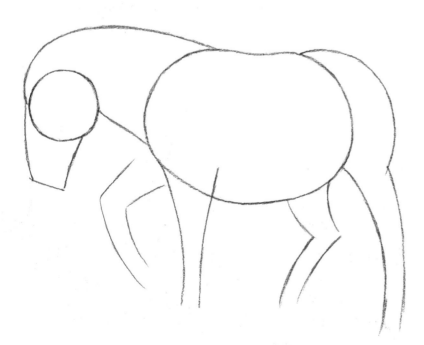

2 Draw the cone shape of the muzzle, and a line to indicate the neck. The neck is wide and strong. The legs are short and thick.

3 Add the details of the ears, mane and tail. Sketch in the big, sturdy leg joints. They are quite close to each other because of the pony's short legs.

4 Draw the main features of the face and sketch in some detail for the mane and tail. Work on the upper parts of the legs, bringing out the curves of the muscles.

SHIPWRECKED PONIES

Chincoteague ponies live on a long island just off the eastern coast of the United States. According to legend, these wild ponies found their way to the island when Spanish ships were wrecked off the coast in the 1500s! But it's more likely that they were brought to the island by farmers, then left to run wild.

ANIMAL FACTS

5 I wanted to make the mane look windswept, so I drew the general flow of its movement. Don't try to put in every detail – it will look more natural to ink and paint the hair in the next stages. I also added a suggestion of scruffy hair around the hooves and lower legs.

6 I inked the flyaway hair in swift strokes with black ink diluted with water. A small amount of ink on the brush allows the texture of the brush hairs to show. I made the general outlines quite rough to capture the shaggy appearance of the pony's coat.

7 Once I had coloured and shaded the animal, I added lots of fine strokes to capture the texture of the coat. This pony's rough coat has little natural sheen, so I kept the highlights to a minimum on the body. I used white ink for the mane and tail and the shaggy legs.

MOORLAND SCENE

Now it's time to test your skills by putting some of the horses in this chapter into a suitable scene. You can choose any of the different kinds of horses we have drawn.

1 When you are creating a scene, it is a good idea to start with a rough version of your artwork. I decided to set two wild ponies against a background scene of windswept moors. I created a rough drawing and worked out a shading scheme, with the light coming from the right-hand side, and a dark, stormy sky.

2 To work out a rough colour scheme, quickly apply some colour to your pencil rough. I chose to use the colours of autumn – yellows, greens and browns, with a heavy purple-grey sky.

3 Once the paint is dry, develop your colour rough with some dark outlining. I decided to make the distant pony dark in colour to stand out against its pale background. I also darkened the sky and some of the shadows, and added a few bright highlights with white ink.

4 On a large sheet of good paper, draw the guidelines for your final picture. Apart from the ponies, there was little detailed drawing required for my scene, but I sketched in the general forms of the landscape.

5 Work some more pencil detail into the scene, including all the marks you will need for inking. I completed the drawings of the ponies and worked on the general textures of the landscape. Rather than draw every stone in the wall, I made marks to guide my inking brush.

6 Now it's time for inking. I inked in the trees over the rough pencil marks, as well as the wall and the grass, all rather loosely. I took more care over the ponies. Then I marked in the distant horizon with a few swift strokes of thinly diluted ink.

7 Before starting on the colour, I worked on the dark areas of the picture. I mixed two shades of dark grey out of blue, dark red and brown. Then I painted them over the sky area with a large brush. I used the same colour for the darker areas of shading on the animals.

8 For the colour, I mixed up several grass colours using greens, browns and yellows. I painted them quickly over the grass, for a feel of rough, scrubby grassland. I darkened the sky and the horse's shadows a little more. Then I worked up the foreground, using more inks, both black and white, to strengthen and develop the various textures.

INSECTS

SHADE AND SHINE

To show an insect's shiny surface you will need to use highlights. You will also need to apply shading to capture the effect of the insect's round body.

With neither shade nor highlights this ladybird looks flat and dull, despite its bright colouring.

Apply shading underneath the main colour. The shading need not be grey – you can use a neutral version of the main colour.

The simplest way to make highlights is to leave parts of the drawing un-inked and unpainted, but you need to plan this carefully.

Here I lifted off the paint using a wet brush and a clean tissue to create highlights. But you can't do this on the black, inked areas.

Adding chalk or pastel highlights on top of a coloured drawing can give good results, but it can be difficult to control the fine details.

The best method for adding highlights is using white ink and a fine-tipped brush. You can water down the ink for a more subtle sheen.

BUTTERFLY

There are many thousands of different types of butterfly and they live in nearly all parts of the world. The striking shapes, colours and patterns of their wings have inspired some beautiful butterfly names, such as 'painted ladies', 'hairstreaks', 'coppers', 'metalmarks' and 'swallowtails'.

1 Butterflies are symmetrical down a centre line, so a grid is a helpful guide to start your picture. Use a ruler to draw two squares side by side. The centre line is where the squares meet. Then draw more guidelines inside the boxes as shown. The lines do not have to be exact, so long as they are the same on each side.

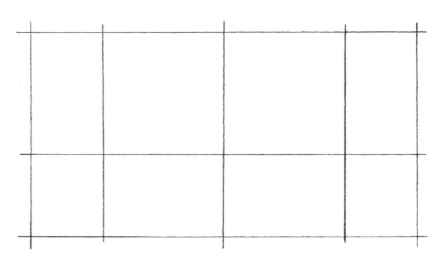

2 Working either side of the centre line, sketch in the three parts of the butterfly's body (head, thorax and abdomen). Add the wing shapes with curves that fit inside the grid guidelines.

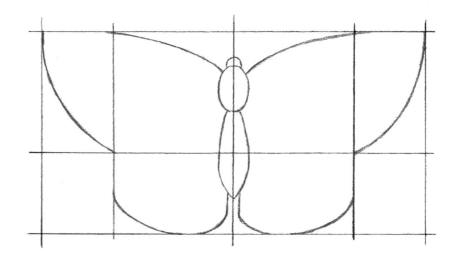

3 Draw the divisions between the wings and then add the outlines of the wing markings, branching out smoothly from the thorax. I decided to draw the two antennae at slightly different angles, to break up the symmetry a bit.

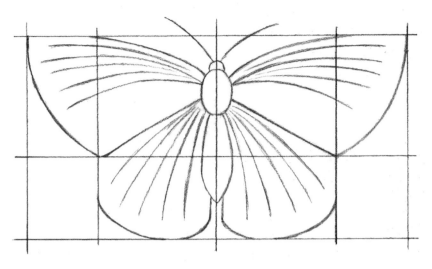

4 Work on the wing markings and the outer shapes of the wings. Then add some detail to the head and mark the curved divisions along the abdomen.

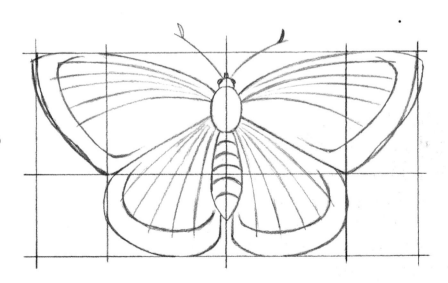

5 The grid lines will help you to place the finer details and markings of the wings symmetrically. Keep going from one side of your picture to the other, making sure each mark is followed by its mirror image.

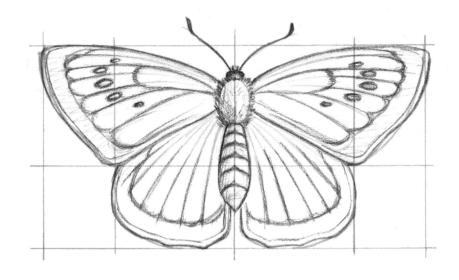

6 For the inking stage, I used a rich blue instead of black, to avoid making the outlines too heavy. I inked in the darker lines of the body and the markings with the tip of a fine brush. Each time the brush started to run dry, I switched to more delicate markings. For the outer edges of the wings, I used tiny strokes of thin brown ink.

7 There is not a lot of shading to be done on a relatively flat subject such as this. But a touch of purple or blue around the body and the inner parts of the wings gives the drawing some solidity and depth.

8 Now apply some colour to the main parts of the wings, to create a pattern. I used some pale pink with a fairly dry brush to stroke a subtle sheen on the inner parts of the wings. For the bolder outer markings I avoided black paint, which would be too heavy here. Instead, I mixed up some brown and blue to make a dark shade.

TINY SCALES

Butterfly wings are covered in tiny scales so minute that the human eye can see them only through a microscope. They help to protect the wings. They also create the beautiful colours and patterns that we see on a butterfly's wings.

ANIMAL FACTS

9 For the main colour, I mixed up a large batch of pale blue. The important thing here is to wash the colour on quickly so as not to disturb the paint you have already put on the wings. Paint with a fairly broad brush, following the direction of the wing markings.

10 For the final detailed touches, I used some white ink and a very fine brush to lift out the delicate highlights of the wing markings. You can also add fine highlights to the fluffy thorax and the shiny abdomen.

HONEY BEE

Bees live on the nectar and pollen produced by flowering plants. Honey bees are a particular type of bee that make honey from the nectar they collect and store it in a honeycomb. Only female bees make honey.

1 Start with the three main body parts: an upside-down egg shape for the head, a circle for the thorax and a large oval for the abdomen. Make sure you leave spaces in between.

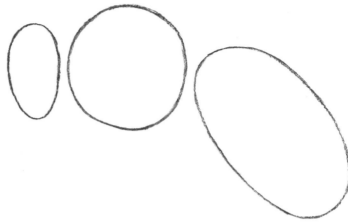

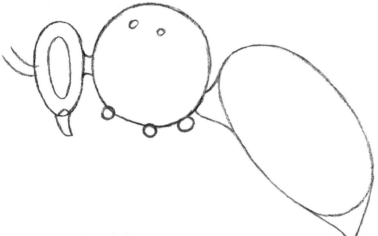

2 Join up the body parts and add the sting at the end of the abdomen. Then draw the large oval eye and the mouth shape. Mark the places where the legs and wings join the thorax with small circles.

DRONES AND WORKERS

Male bees, or drones, don't collect nectar or pollen. It's up to the female worker bees to do all the hard work – collecting nectar, cleaning up and guarding the hive (the bees' home). Queen honey bees rule the hive, and can lay up to 2,000 eggs in one day!

ANIMAL FACTS

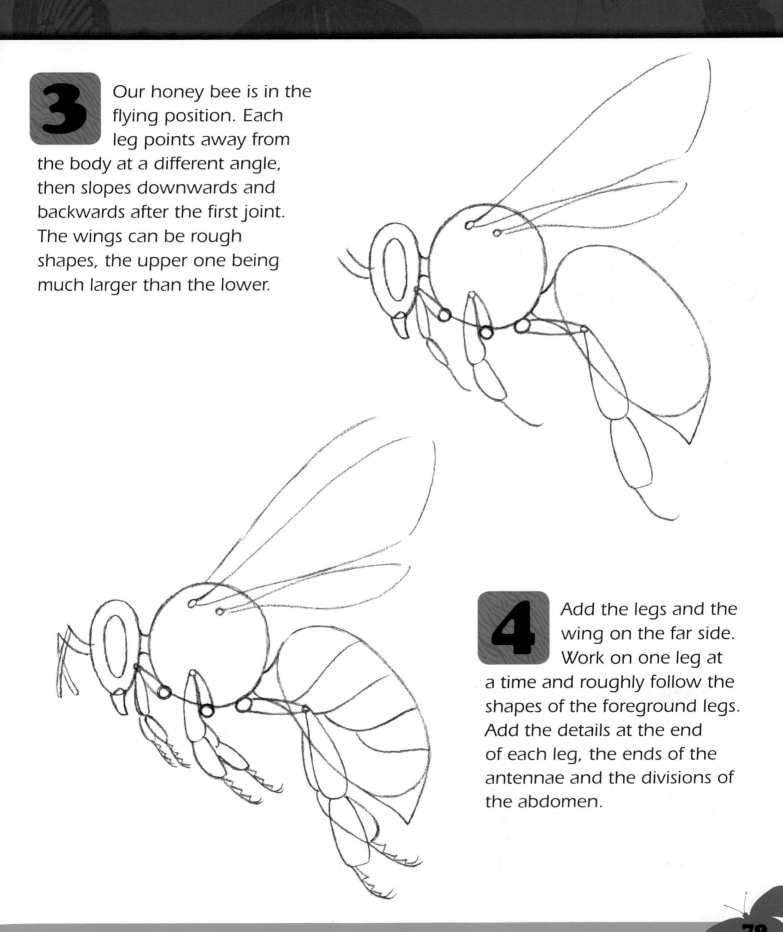

3 Our honey bee is in the flying position. Each leg points away from the body at a different angle, then slopes downwards and backwards after the first joint. The wings can be rough shapes, the upper one being much larger than the lower.

4 Add the legs and the wing on the far side. Work on one leg at a time and roughly follow the shapes of the foreground legs. Add the details at the end of each leg, the ends of the antennae and the divisions of the abdomen.

5 Now work on the details, particularly the characteristic fluffy texture of the thorax, which increases its size on the page. Add more fluffy marks around the head.

6 For the inking stage, use black ink in firm strokes for the hard parts of the abdomen and the legs. Use lots of soft strokes for the furry parts and the fast-moving wings, and fine hatched lines for the eye.

7 To colour the bee, I used layers of browns and yellows for the thorax and head, to build up a textured feel. The blurry wings needed only a few swift strokes. The abdomen took rather longer, as I blended black stripes into the yellow. For the highlights I used tiny, soft strokes for the fluffy parts and bold, shiny marks for the smooth abdomen.

COUNTRY SCENE

Now it's time to bring together the skills you have learned in this chapter and put your insects into a countryside scene. I chose a bank of wildflowers as a suitable background scene for butterflies and bees. I did lots of small, rough drawings before selecting one to work up in greater detail.

1 When you are creating a scene, it is a good idea to start with a rough version of your artwork. To allow for close-up drawings of the insects, I chose a low eye level. This means that the fence is above eye level, disappearing towards the distant horizon. A cottage provides some interest.

2 Next, I quickly washed on some watercolours to establish a rough colour scheme. I also decided on a light source – bright sunshine coming from the right – and shaded the scene with that in mind.

3 Still working on my colour rough, I used dark ink to strengthen parts of the drawing and white ink to make some features clearer. I decided that the top right part of the picture was a little empty, so I added more trees. I also added a patch of shade to the road, to provide a darker background behind the flowers.

4 Use your colour rough as a guide to map out your scene on good paper. First I established the curves that run through the picture and the main features of the drawing. The aim of this stage is to place the elements on the page, so everything can be drawn quite loosely.

5 Much of the detail in this scene will be added in the inking and painting stages. There's no need to draw each blade of grass. However, the cottage and the insects need good guidelines if they are to look convincing. It is also important to get the spacing right between the fence posts, to give a sense of distance.

6 Next add detail to the insects and cottage, as well as the larger flowers. The flowers need not be precisely detailed, but they should have some individual characteristics.

7 For the inking stage, I decided to use very little black ink, keeping it for just the insects to make them stand out. To create a bright picture, I inked the foliage with green, the poppies with dark red and the wooden details with dark brown. I used some strokes of purple watercolour for a faint horizon.

8 Using my colour rough, I was able to add colour and shade quite quickly and confidently. Once the main colours were blocked in, I mixed white ink into yellows and greens to layer some lighter grass over darker areas. I mixed white in with red for highlights on the poppies. Then I added some daisies on top of the grass.

SEA CREATURES

TIPS AND TRICKS

DOLPHIN SHAPES

Here are some tips for drawing a dolphin from several different viewpoints.

The same approach can be used for many other creatures found in the oceans. The details and proportions may vary, but they can be drawn using the same basic shapes.

A better angle of view shows the front and side at the same time. It is much like the side-on view, except that the oval and tail are more squashed.

This diagram shows the dolphin side-on. The shape can be broken down into a long oval and a pointed tail, with the nose and fins added on.

This is similar to the previous viewpoint, but the dolphin appears to be closer. The face is larger and the tail smaller.

Seen from the front, the basic shape is little more than a circle. It is difficult to make this look real.

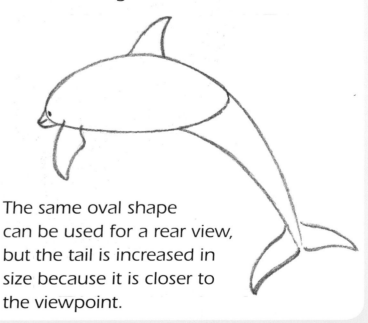

The same oval shape can be used for a rear view, but the tail is increased in size because it is closer to the viewpoint.

DOLPHIN

Dolphins live in the world's warmer seas and oceans, usually in groups known as 'pods'. These are bottlenose dolphins – they are called that because their long snouts look rather like bottles! They can vary in colour from light bluish-grey to almost black.

1 I decided to draw a pair of dolphins swimming together. You can, of course, choose to draw only one. The body shape of the main dolphin is two curves meeting at a broadly rounded head. The other dolphin is a long oval with a separate tail.

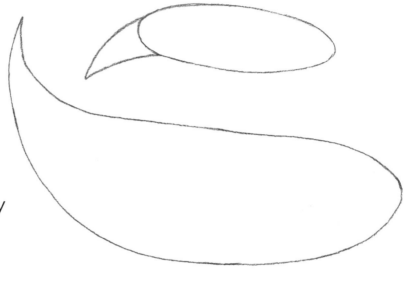

2 Add the shapes of the snouts, one closed and the other open. The tail fins start as simple triangles. Make sure these triangles fit symmetrically on to the body.

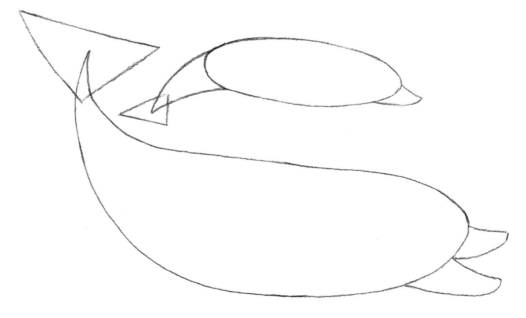

3 Draw the back fins and flippers. Note that the back fins sit to the rear of the bodies. Add mouth openings that extend into the head – these will help you to position the eyes.

4 Shape the tail fins neatly within the triangles. Then work on the other fins, rounding off the corners and blending them smoothly into the bodies. Complete the snout shapes with curved lines where the upper jaw joins the head.

5 Make sure your drawings are sleek and streamlined, and erase any confusing guidelines. Because the shapes of these animals are quite simple, you need to be careful with every outline.

6 For the inking stage, try to ink each part of your drawing with continuous, unbroken lines. Use a fine but well-loaded brush, so that the ink doesn't run out halfway along a graceful curve. Make the outline slightly broader on the shaded undersides and finer along the upper surfaces.

7 Even simple colouring like that of the dolphin requires several stages to be really effective. Work on the shading first. For this picture I used a blue-grey colour. Before each section dried, I softened the edges with a wet brush to blend the dark parts into the light, to suggest smoothly rounded bodies.

DOLPHIN SENSES

Dolphins are highly intelligent creatures. When they are hunting, they make clicking sounds and then listen for the echo of the sound as it bounces back. The time it takes for the sound to return tells the dolphin how far away its prey is. This is called echolocation. Dolphins also 'talk' to each other with a wide range of whistles and other sounds.

ANIMAL FACTS

8 Now add the plain grey colouring. For this I mixed some golden brown into the grey. Mix up plenty of paint so you don't run out halfway through the painting. I painted this layer in swift, broad strokes and softened the bottom edges to blend into the pale undersides.

9 To bring some roundness to the shapes of the dolphins, and to show where the light falls, I lightened the upper surfaces. I used a soft, damp brush to moisten the paint and lift it off the surface, cleaning the brush frequently.

10 For the final touches, I diluted white ink with water to pick out the delicate highlights on the upper parts, and to neaten up the mouth and eye areas. Then I mixed some blue into the white ink to paint some fine strips of colour on to the dolphins' undersides.

SEAHORSE

These strange little creatures look like miniature horses – that's where their name comes from. However, they are in fact bony fish. They swim upright in some of the world's warm seas and oceans by fluttering the small fins on their backs. To rest, they attach themselves to corals or sea grasses with their long, spiral tails.

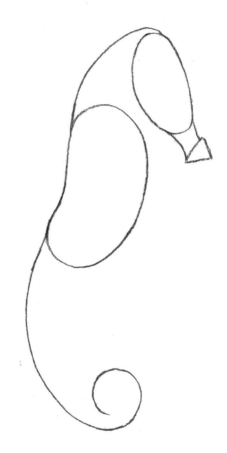

1 Start the seahorse's long head and body with two slightly squashed ovals. The head should be quite flat on top and more rounded underneath. The body dips in at the back, in a bean shape.

2 Join the two ovals with an arching line for the outside of the neck. The tail begins as a long curve that runs from the back and ends in a loose spiral. Add in the triangular nose part.

SEAHORSE SNACKS

Seahorses use their long snouts to suck in tiny sea creatures for food. They have no teeth and no stomach! This means that seahorses must feed almost constantly in order to process enough food to keep them alive.

ANIMAL FACTS

3 Draw the inside line of the tail, which forms a tight spiral at the end. Add facial features and fins around the jawline and in the middle of the back.

4 Mark some guidelines for the ridges on the seahorse's body. Take care to make them regular in size on the body, and smaller as you work down the tail.

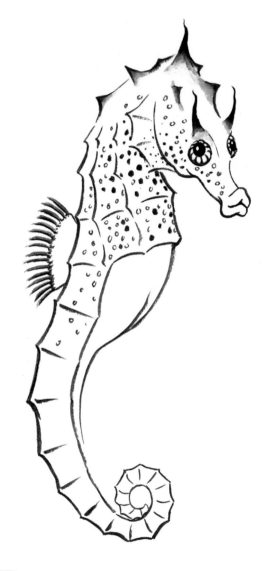

5 Now you can refine your drawing, adding detail and texture to the guidelines. Work on the ridges of the body to give them some depth. Then spend some time working on the features of the face, and the back fin.

6 For such a delicate and colourful creature, I chose a warm red-brown colour for the inking stage. I used black ink for the eyes and the tips of the horns. I also added some small dots and circles around the face and chest.

7 Like many fish, seahorses come in a remarkable range of colours and markings. Some are dull brown and grey, but I chose a more colourful example. I used orange and yellow, blending into a greenish tint around the face. White highlights help to bring out the various ridges and bumps on the seahorse's body.

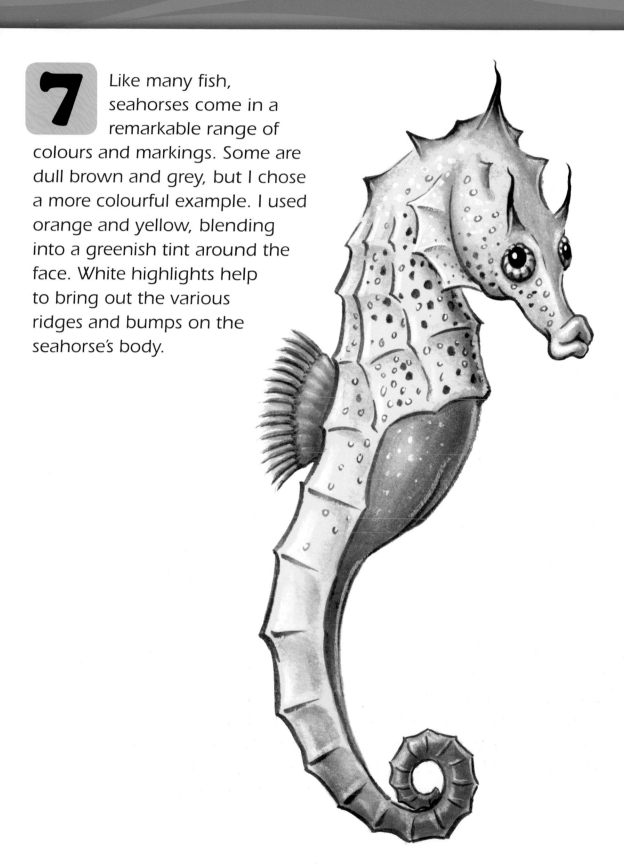

UNDERWATER SCENE

Now it's time to bring together the skills you have learned in this chapter to place your sea creatures against a suitable background. I decided to use an underwater scene, with two dolphins swimming near a sunken wreck.

1 I found lots of photos of underwater scenes and started to think about a suitable setting. Working roughly on a small sheet of paper I arranged the boat so that it echoes the shape of the leading dolphin and makes a sweeping curve through the picture.

2 To work out the shading and colouring, I washed some colours directly on to my pencil rough. I used purply-blue for the shadow areas and deep water, then yellows, oranges and greens for the coral, plants and the rusty wreck. For the open water, I used a paler turquoise blue.

3 Still working on my colour rough, I strengthened the outlines and shadows of the dolphins, coral and plants in the foreground with black ink and more purply-blue paint. I also added some highlights with white ink. To make the scene livelier, I worked in a number of small fish, some as distant, dark shapes, and some in bright yellow in the foreground.

4 On a large sheet of good paper, I mapped out the basic shapes of the drawing in pencil. At this stage, I decided to add some extra dolphins in the background.

5 I worked up the details of the drawing over the rough guidelines, still in pencil. I didn't put in too much detail for the corals and weeds, as this can be added directly at the inking stage.

6 For the inking, I mainly used blue ink to create the effect of looking through water. I made the outlines more and more dark towards the foreground, switching to black ink for the corals and plants, and the nearest dolphin. Once the ink was dry, I erased all the pencil marks.

7 Before applying any colour, I painted all the shading and shadow areas. I used pale, diluted blue for the distant parts, darker blue in the middle ground, and black shadows in the foreground.

8 To colour the scene, I started by filling in the solid blue of the sea, darker at the sea floor and paler towards the surface. I then roughly coloured all the other parts with browns, oranges and greens, and grey for the dolphins. Once all the paper was covered, I mixed white ink into the colours to pick out textures and highlight edges. I also used a few touches of pure white ink for highlights in the foreground.

BIG CATS

HEADS AND FACES

To draw the face of any cat, try thinking of it as an upside-down triangle with a rough circle for the head and fur.

Basic shape

The pattern is very similar for all of the cats. Only the proportions are different.

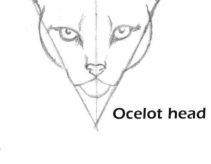

Ocelot head

Cougar head

The circle is obvious in the rounded head of a cougar. All of the cougar's features fit within the triangle except for its muzzle.

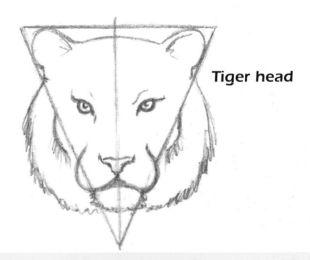

Tiger head

TIGER SKULL

It is useful for artists to have a basic understanding of what lies beneath the surface of the creatures they draw.

The tiger's skull reveals the awesome size of its teeth.

Tiger skull

When the tiger's face is drawn over the top of the skull, you can see that the main features (mouth, nose and eyes) are in quite a small central area.

TIGER

The largest of the big cats, the tiger is a strong and ferocious hunter. Its beautiful striped coat makes it difficult to spot in the grasslands and forests that are its home.

1 Although the tiger is a strong and thick-set animal, its body shape is in fact quite slender. Begin with a long oval and make it bow slightly in the middle. Mark a neat circle at the front end for the basic head shape.

2 Draw curving lines around the head to mark the centre of the face and the level of the eyes. Add in the lines of the powerful upper legs.

3 Develop the face by drawing guidelines for the muzzle, including a centre line running through both the upper and lower jaws. Extend the legs with the more angular shapes of the ankles and add some contours on the top edge to indicate the curve of the neck and protruding shoulders.

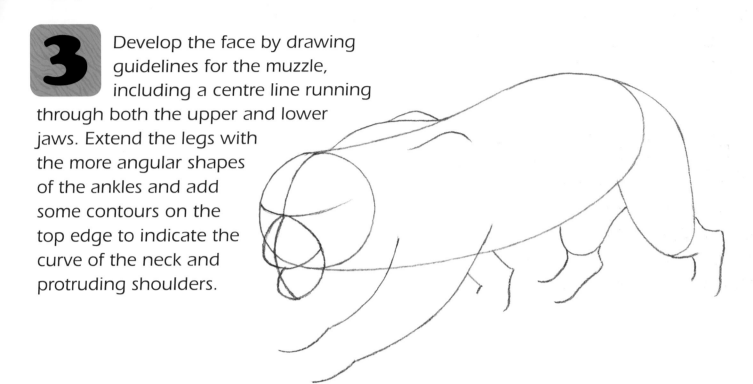

4 Copy the main features of the tiger's face, not forgetting the distinctive fur ruff around its jaw line. Add the toes, making sure they overlap each other convincingly. Then give your tiger a long, elegant tail.

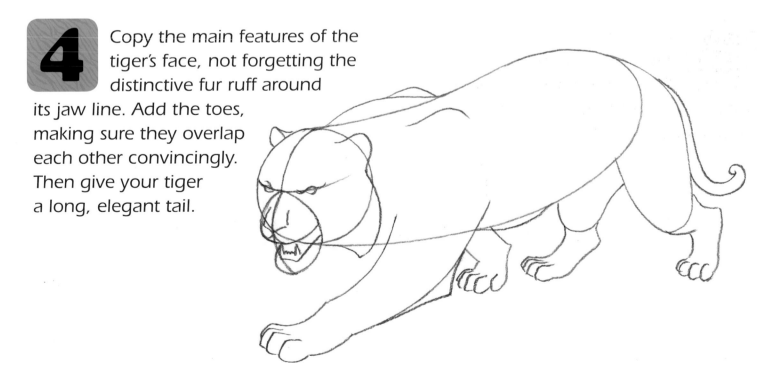

5 With the guidelines all established you can now enjoy working on the fine detail. Switch to a softer pencil and make sure it is sharp. Include a centre line down the tiger's back and some rough guidelines for the curves and spacings of the stripes.

6 For the inking stage, keep the outlines smooth and simple, allowing the brush to vary the weight of the lines. Use the tip of the brush, lightly loaded, to ink the eyes, mouth and nose. The black claws can be inked with single strokes. Don't erase the guidelines yet, as you will need them for the markings.

7 The tiger's markings are black stripes, so I have done them in ink. Work either side of the centre guidelines down the tiger's back and head to make the stripes symmetrical, and give them a rough, hairy texture. Don't do too many – leave some space in between each stripe.

COOL CATS

Unlike many cats, tigers love water. In the heat of the day, tigers often choose to cool off by taking a dip in lakes or streams. With their powerful bodies and webbed paws, tigers are strong swimmers. They can cover many kilometres in the water, crossing rivers or chasing prey.

ANIMAL FACTS

8 With your watercolours, mix up some watery grey using dark blue, red and maybe a touch of brown. Be sure you have decided the direction of the light – here it is coming from the upper right. Then apply some shading to the parts facing away from the light.

9 Mix some red and brown to make orange and paint the upper back, face and shoulders. Once it is dry, use an orangey brown to paint across the entire coloured area, which will blend the darker orange with the new colour. Remember to leave white patches on the face, belly and tail.

10 To finish the painting, add patches of colour to the eyes and mouth. Then put in any extra shading or richer colour that seems necessary. Use a fine brush and white ink to paint delicate highlights around the teeth, nose and ears and to add some very fine whiskers.

LION

The lion is king of the animals, with powerful legs for chasing prey. The male lion has a thick mane of hair around his neck. This bushy mane makes the lion look larger, which helps to frighten off rivals. The mane also protects the lion's neck during fights.

1 Start with the lion's head by drawing a triangle, point downwards. Position the triangle to the right of the page. Then draw a long egg shape, almost touching it. Leave enough space around the shapes to fit the rest of the lion on your paper. Look at the example to make sure your shapes are the right sizes in relation to each other.

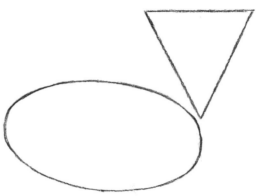

2 Next, you can add the strong upper parts of the lion's legs. Draw four long ovals, being careful to pay attention to the sizes and how they fit onto the body. You can then join up the chest and the hips with curved lines.

HUNTERS

Many lions live in groups called prides. While the male lions protect the pride's territory, it is the lionesses (female lions) that do most of the hunting for food. They are smaller and more agile than the males, and they often work together to kill their prey.

3 Complete the basic lion shape with the powerful lower legs and the tail. Draw in a rough outline for the mane. Mark a centre line down the lion's head, and a line across at the level of the eyes.

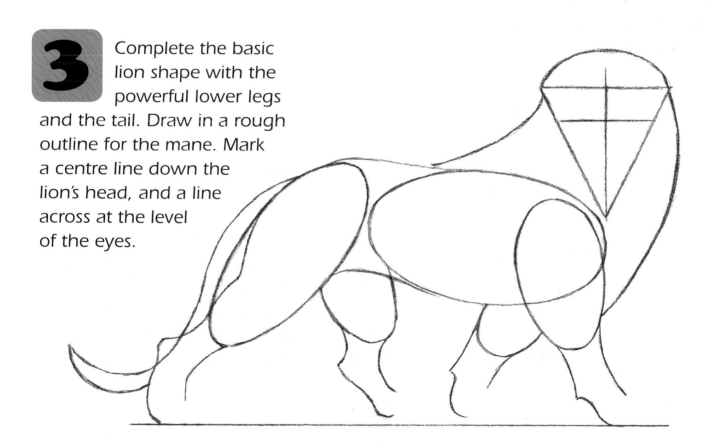

4 Continue to work on the lion's face. Use the guidelines to make sure the mouth, nose and eyes are symmetrical. Then draw the ears and add some texture to the outline of the mane. Draw the feet as individual rounded toes.

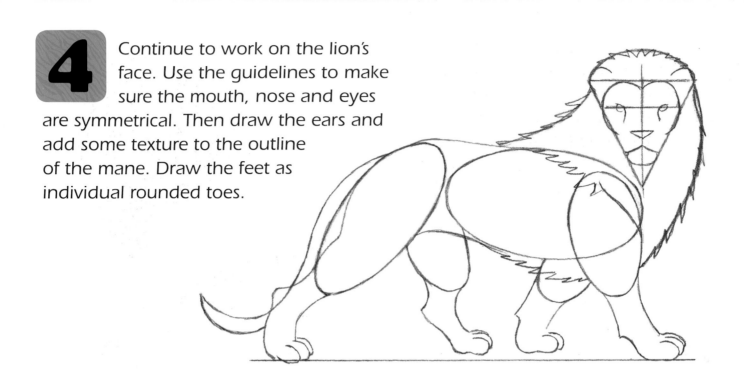

5 Now the basic lion shape is complete, you can start to look at the details. At this stage it's a good idea to work some texture into the mane to guide your ink drawing. You can also plan where the shading will appear on the lion's body.

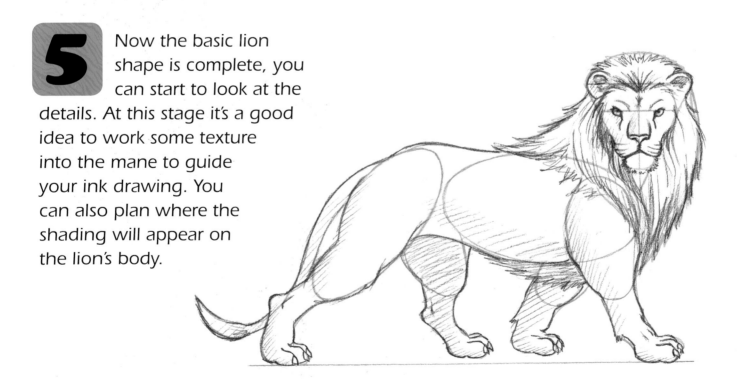

6 Apart from the mane, the lion has a smooth coat. Use black ink to create a smooth and graceful outline that brings out the animal's muscular build. The mane has a scruffier texture. Ink in the texture but don't overdo it – leave some space for the colour.

7 You might think a lion is the same sandy colour all over, but in fact its coat is darker and more orange across its back and on its tail and nose. The mane is also darker and slightly redder.

JAGUAR

The jaguar is the largest cat in Central and South America. It is a swift and agile hunter with a very powerful bite. Its name means 'one that kills with one leap'.

1 Start with a circle for the jaguar's head. The oval of the body has a shallow curve running up the back and a deeper curve to follow the more rounded tummy.

2 Start the rear end by extending the curve of the back around the rump and into the rear thigh. The front leg should be drawn right up into the shoulder and arched over the back. The guidelines should already have a solid, cat-like form.

3 Now add the foot shapes and tail. Then draw a centre line that wraps around the head, neck, shoulders and back.

4 Draw in the main features of the head, working on either side of the centre line for symmetry. The toes should be strong and well-rounded. Add some curves around the tail to make it look rounded too.

5 Refine the drawing by adding more detail to the features, including the claws. A little shading will really help at the next stage. The downward motion of this pose requires a surface for the jaguar to be walking on. I've chosen a broad tree branch, but you could place your jaguar on rocks or rough ground.

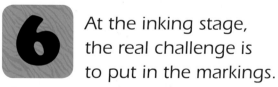

6 At the inking stage, the real challenge is to put in the markings. Start at the head by adding small spots, mirrored on either side of the centre line. Make the spots larger as you work over the shoulders and back. Allow the markings to follow the curves across the body, getting slimmer around the shoulder, tummy and rump.

CLIMBING CATS

The jaguar stalks its prey before attacking with one deadly pounce. Jaguars are good at climbing trees and they are also excellent swimmers.

ANIMAL FACTS

7 The jaguar's colouring is quite simple – just a little richer across the top of the head, inside the ring markings and around the rear end. Leave the paws and lower face pale. Then concentrate on making the ground surface look natural. Some highlights may be helpful here.

JUNGLE SCENE

Learning how to draw and paint animals is just a step along the way to making finished pictures. A bigger challenge is to set your animals against a background that brings out their natural behaviour. Here are some of the steps I took to create a scene for the jaguar. You may choose to work with a different cat, or on a less complicated background.

1 After trying out many different compositions very roughly, I decided on this one and drew it quickly on scrap paper. The aim is to work out how the parts of the scene fit together, and be able to make alterations without messing up a detailed drawing.

2 Working on top of my rough pencil drawing, I added some shade and colour in broad blocks of watercolour. This helped me to see how the composition works.

3 Using black and white inks, I developed the lights and darks of the scene. I decided to make the foreground tree largely dark, showing in silhouette against the background. The ruined building is lighter against the darker background. I also decided to add another toucan.

4 On a larger sheet of heavier paper, start your artwork by drafting the main shapes and guidelines. The important principle here is to work broadly without any details at this stage.

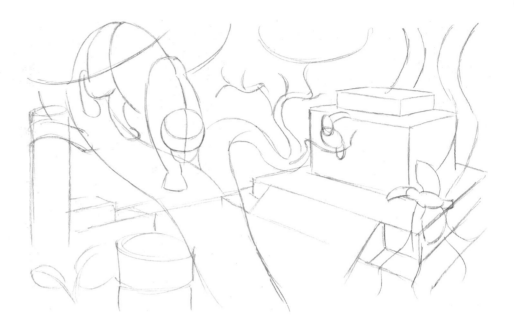

5 Gradually develop the details, bringing form to the rough masses. Although I intended the building to be a ruin, I drew it as a complete shape first so that it would look convincing.

6 Use a softer pencil to complete the detailed drawing. Erase your guidelines as you go. I have left some of the detail sketchy, allowing some possibility for development in the ink and colour stages.

7 As I inked in the various lines and textures I decided that the main tree shape wasn't quite right, so I added another branch. When inking, it's important to keep in mind the light source and shading, and to add the appropriate texture to each surface.

8 Because I had worked out most of the light and shade decisions with my coloured rough (stage 2), I could apply the shading and colours to my ink drawing with confidence. A few highlights helped to bring out the details of the various plants.

WHY NOT TRY?

Now that you have practised all your new techniques, why not try some other animals? Have a look at the ideas below, or pick your own!

WILD HORSE

COBRA

CHEETAH